"Any sufficiently advanced technology is indistinguishable from magic."

Arthur C. Clarke

Copyright © 2025

by The Center Lane Project

THE 12 PRINCIPLES OF REMOTE VIEWING
*A Clear Guide to the Foundations
of the Remote Viewing Method*

Jana Rogge
The Center Lane Project

co-authored by
John P. Stahler
Lily Fowler
Jon Noble
Hakim Isler

The principles described here apply to remote viewing in general, regardless of the form and method. Controlled Remote Viewing (CRV) has additional features like its structure that distinguish it from other, less disciplined forms of remote viewing.

CENTER LANE was one of the code names of the Military Remote Viewing programme, covering the 1983–1984 period, the time when Ingo Swann trained 5 Military remote viewers — Tom McNear, Bill Ray, Paul H. Smith, Charlene Cavanaugh (Shufelt) and Ed Dames — in the CRV method that he had developed together with Hal Puthoff.

The Center Lane Project is a non-profit, 501(c)(3) organization dedicated to transfer the knowledge and principles about original CRV and Remote Viewing history to the next generation.

WWW.CENTERLANE-RV.ORG

THE 12 PRINCIPLES *OF* REMOTE VIEWING

A CLEAR GUIDE TO THE FOUNDATIONS OF THE REMOTE VIEWING METHOD

THE CENTER LANE PROJECT

CONTENTS

Foreword by Jana Rogge 3

Abstract 9
Where Does Remote Viewing Come From? 10
Previous Definitions of Remote Viewing 12
Remote Viewing "In the Wild" 13

THE REMOTE VIEWING PRINCIPLES

1	Trainable Skill	13
2	Always Intentional	14
3	Controlled Target Access	14
4	Bilocation Balance	14
5	Blinding Protocols	16
6	Concept of Mental Noise	17
7	Descriptive Reporting	18
8	Defined Working Structure	18
9	Recording in Real Time	20
10	Process-Related Data	21
11	Feedback	22
12	Redundancy	22

Comparison to Different Modes of Psychic Work 24
Signatures and Endorsements 26

REMOTE VIEWING GLOSSARY

Remote Viewing Glossary 29
The CLP Target Library 47
Genealogy of Remote Viewing 48

THE PRINCIPLES OF REMOTE VIEWING

FOREWORD
JANA ROGGE

Jana Rogge, president of The Center Lane Project

When we founded the *Center Lane Project* in 2023, our goal was to create a non-profit organization dedicated to preserving and transferring the original knowledge and principles of Controlled Remote Viewing (CRV) to future generations. We were motivated by concerns that the foundational methods and teachings of CRV—developed by Ingo Swann and Hal Puthoff and taught to a small group of military viewers in the 1980s—were at risk of being lost or diluted as the field expanded and new, often modified, remote viewing methods proliferated after the original programs were declassified in 1995.

The project aims to capture the essence of CRV, ensure its core principles are not obscured by later innovations, and make this body of knowledge accessible for education and research. It also seeks to support both newcomers and experienced practitioners by providing reliable resources and fostering a network for knowledge sharing and practitioner support.

Anyone who has taken a closer look at the topic will agree that the knowledge of remote viewing is inseparably intertwined with

RV's history—just as it is in other areas of life. Those who understand the history, the processes, and the chronology of each development can truly grasp the method and its theoretical, scientific, and practical foundations.

That's why we decided to also include the entire historical context of remote viewing in our project, making the knowledge accessible to interested individuals and new remote viewers.

Unlike our general work that focuses exclusively on Controlled Remote Viewing (CRV), this booklet deliberately addresses Remote Viewing (RV) in its broadest sense, independent of any particular school or methodology.

People find their way to remote viewing through a wide variety of paths, each bringing its own perspective and expectations. For some, the journey begins with books, reports and interviews featuring the original viewers from the military unit, whose stories have reached a certain presence in media and documentaries. Others first encounter remote viewing in adjacent communities, such as among UFO/UAP enthusiasts, anomaly researchers, or those interested in out-of-body experiences, where the topic is often discussed alongside other extraordinary phenomena.

Some are introduced to remote viewing through courses at the Monroe Institute, which focus on exploring altered states of consciousness. These courses have helped popularize the idea in broader circles. There are also psychics who market their services as remote viewing, even though what they offer may differ significantly from the structured methods developed in the original programs. At the same time, genuine remote viewers who openly share their work or offer training play a crucial role in attracting newcomers and passing on their knowledge.

In recent years, the proliferation of YouTube videos and documentaries about mysteries and secret government projects—often highlighting the U.S. government's involvement in remote viewing—has further fueled public curiosity. This diversity of entry points has led to a wide range of interpretations and expectations, making it all the more important to clarify what remote viewing truly is and how it differs from other practices in the field of psi phenomena.

A major issue that has emerged over time is that the term "remote viewing" has gradually evolved into a catch-all buzzword for a wide array of psi phenomena, regardless of their actual connection to the original protocol and methodology. This misuse is partly driven by the desire for borrowed legitimacy; Its scientific origins and structured protocols of remote viewing lend remote viewing an air of credibility that is often lacking in other areas of popular parapsychology. In a field frequently met with skepticism or outright dismissal, adopting the label "remote viewing" can make practices seem more serious and research-based, especially since terms like "clairvoyance" or "psychic" are often associated with unscientific or mystical connotations.

Additionally, many people simply lack a clear understanding of what truly distinguishes remote viewing from other forms of extrasensory perception (ESP). The original remote viewing protocols were developed through years of research and refinement, emphasizing repeatability, documentation, and a strict separation between the viewer and the target. In contrast, many who use the term today may be unaware of these rigorous standards, and instead apply the remote viewing term to any intuitive or psychic process involving information gathering at a distance.

The widespread use of "remote viewing" as a marketing term also plays a role. Some psychics and intuitives rebrand their services under this label to attract clients who are seeking something with a scientific or military pedigree. This further blurs the lines between genuine remote viewing and other, less rigorous psychic practices. As a result, the public's understanding of what remote viewing actually entails becomes muddled, making it harder for newcomers to discern authentic methods from loosely related or entirely unrelated practices. This confusion underscores the importance of clear definitions and education about the unique features and history of remote viewing.

The earliest written definitions of remote viewing provide only limited guidance for understanding what truly sets this discipline apart. In the initial years of research, the terminology and concepts surrounding remote viewing were still evolving, as the primary focus at that time was on providing evidence for the existence of ESP. It was only about a decade later that efforts shifted toward the development of a structured training methodology for remote viewing. The distinctions that now separate it from other forms of extrasensory perception were not yet fully established. As the field matured, through systematic experimentation and practical application, the protocols and criteria that define remote viewing were gradually developed and refined.

Today, when we compare those early, broad definitions with the much deeper understanding held by trained remote viewers of the second or third generation, the importance of clear and precise descriptions becomes evident.

FOREWORD

To address this need, we have worked closely with our group of advisors, all of whom were key figures in the development of remote viewing: Hal Puthoff, the lead scientist of the original RV program; Skip Atwater, the operations and training officer of the military remote viewing unit at Ft. Meade; and three of the first and original CRV viewers from that unit—Tom McNear, Paul H. Smith, and Bill Ray, who also served several years as the unit's commander. Together, with their unique expertise and first-hand experience, we have distilled the essential features that truly characterize remote viewing.

The result is a set of guiding principles that provide a reliable framework for identifying and practicing remote viewing, regardless of the specific method used.

These **Principles of Remote Viewing** are designed to be universally applicable—not limited to Controlled Remote Viewing (CRV), but relevant to any approach that genuinely embodies the core aspects of RV, now and in the future as the field continues to evolve.

This booklet serves as a compact guide and orientation for anyone interested in remote viewing. It brings together the essential basics and the most important definitions—information you won't find presented in such a concise form anywhere else. Whether you're new to the topic, looking for clear foundations, or simply want a quick reference, *Principles of Remote Viewing* offers a uniquely accessible introduction to the core concepts of the field.

Jana Rogge
President, Center Lane Project
June 2025

THE PRINCIPLES OF REMOTE VIEWING

INTRODUCTION

ABSTRACT

Remote viewing is a disciplined method that trains individuals to obtain information about distant or concealed objects, events, locations, or people beyond normal sensory capabilities. Developed and utilized by both scientific research and military intelligence, it involves structured protocols to enhance and control psychic functioning, distinct from other psychic practices. Remote viewing is based on the human ability of Extrasensory Perception (ESP), and includes some mechanism or procedure for controlling mental noise.

We can identify **12 principles** to distinguish remote viewing (in general) from other psychic disciplines. This book discusses these 12 principles of remote viewing.

THE PRINCIPLES OF REMOTE VIEWING

Remote viewing is a technique used to obtain information that is not available otherwise through normal senses or information sources, separated from us by space, time, or shielding.

Remote viewing is not clairvoyance, channeling, out-of-body or other mediumistic work, but it is related to such techniques in that it utilizes the natural human capacity for extrasensory perception. Therefore, remote viewing does not refer to the ability to psychically perceive things itself, but is a technique to develop, strengthen and make controlled use of psychic functioning.

WHERE DOES REMOTE VIEWING COME FROM?

The term "remote viewing" was coined by artist and psychic Ingo Swann in the early 1970s. He participated in scientific studies of Extrasensory Perception (ESP) at the American Society for Psychical Research (ASPR), the City College in New York, and Stanford Research Institute (SRI). It was subsequently adopted by US military intelligence for a secret psychic espionage program that ran until 1995, involving various US government agencies including the CIA and DIA. After it was declassified and publicly revealed in 1995, the program became famous as the "Star Gate" Program, referring to one of its code names.

Based on an extended research program led by physicists Hal Puthoff and Russell Targ at SRI, and after about a decade of studies with both natural psychics and individuals without reported psychic abilities or prior psychic claims, it became evident that non-local perception—the ability to describe distant places, objects, people or events not accessible through regular sensory means—

INTRODUCTION

was potentially an inherent human ability that could be developed and trained like any other human capacity.

Similar to the working method applied for scientific studies, the US government and military used a generic remote viewing approach in different programs from 1975 onward. But beginning from 1981, a formalized and structured working method called *Coordinate Remote Viewing* (CRV, later known as *Controlled Remote Viewing*) was developed at SRI by Ingo Swann and Hal Puthoff. This method was trained and used by a small group of military remote viewers in the secret psychic spy unit, based at Ft. Meade, Maryland. After the program was terminated and publicly disclosed in 1995, some of the former military personnel began teaching the method in the civilian world. Through these instructors and subsequently their students, a variety of adaptions to remote viewing are available today as training for individuals, ranging from „free form" approaches to structured, method-based written formats.

Although there are now many different approaches that share the name "remote viewing," there are clear indications that distinguish remote viewing from other psychic practices, such as clairvoyance, channeling, astral projection, or out-of-body experiences.

THE PRINCIPLES OF REMOTE VIEWING

DEFINITION OF REMOTE VIEWING (DIA)
Remote Viewing is the acquisition and description, by mental means, of information blocked from ordinary perception by distance, shielding or time.

(Coordinate Remote Viewing, Defense Intelligence Agency, 1 May 1986)

DEFINITION OF REMOTE VIEWING (IRVA)
RV is a novel perceptual discipline for gaining information not available to the ordinary physical senses. Used extensively by so-called "psychic spies" during the Cold War for classified military projects, it has a long history both as an intelligence gathering tool and as the subject of research and applications in the civilian world.

(International Remote Viewing Association, IRVA.org)

ABOUT REMOTE VIEWING (INGO SWANN)
[The term remote viewing] was coined to identify a particular kind of experiment—not a particular kind of psi ability. To simplify all this, we can resort to a easy-to-understand formula. Remote-viewing consists of five absolutely necessary ingredients: (1) subject, [with] (2) active ESP abilities, [directed at] (3) distant target [including shielded or distant in time] (4) subject's recorded responses and (5) confirmatory positive feedback, all of which equals (6) the remote-viewing model. Nothing less is remote viewing. [...] Remote-viewing is neither a novel psi ability, nor a convenient replacement term for psi, clairvoyance, or ESP.

(Ingo Swann, in Fate Magazine, Sept 1993)

REMOTE VIEWING "IN THE WILD"

Over the past three decades, the term "remote viewing" has become a catch-all phrase for many psychic practices, largely because the scientific framework of the method appeals to those seeking greater public acceptance of psychic abilities and the paranormal. Additionally, the term "viewing" is misleading, further contributing to misconceptions about what remote viewing actually entails (which is discussed below in this text). As a result, today the majority of people using this terminology have a flawed understanding of its true meaning and principles.

THE REMOTE VIEWING PRINCIPLES

In the following, twelve main characteristics (principles) of remote viewing vs. other psychic work are discussed in a short form.

1

Remote viewing is a trainable skill, based on an innate human ability.

The ability to perform remote viewing is acquired through practice and experience in the method—in short, anyone can become a remote viewer. Remote viewing does not require that one have a "gift" or talent as in other "psychic" or mediumistic approaches. As with any human skill set, an innate talent may give a person some advantage. But quality training and consistent practise is more important for developing a professional skill level. Proper training and experience can augment talent and compensate for a lesser amount of natural talent.

THE PRINCIPLES OF REMOTE VIEWING

2
Remote viewing is always an intentional (deliberate) process.

Remote viewing does not occur spontaneously or without intention. It is performed for a specific pre-defined purpose, in the form of "sessions" with a start and end point defined and recorded by the viewer and always involves intentional directed awareness.

3
Control of the process of mentally accessing a remote viewing target belongs to the viewer.

The viewer chooses whether to remote view an assigned target, as well as when to do so. Even though always blinded to the target (see Principle 5, below), it is the viewer who decides whether to work on this specific target, and when to start and end the process. During their sessions, viewers may freely change their perspective around and about the target both in time and space as they feel necessary to accomplish the purpose of the assignment.

In essence, the viewer is in charge. If present, a monitor may only offer guidance as a suggestion, not a requirement.

4
Bilocation (balanced perception) is essential.

The word "bilocation" literally means being in two places at the same time. But the word has more than one interpretation. For example, it can mean being physically in two locations simultaneously, in the way that certain Catholic saints were reported as having been seen at two widely-separated locations at the same time. It is not this kind of bilocation we are talking about in remote viewing. In remote viewing it means something different.

According to the originator of remote viewing, Ingo Swann, bilocation means that during a remote viewing session, the viewer maintains a balance between being aware of being "here" in the remote viewing room and, at the same time, aware of being "there" at the target. Instead of the viewer's body or visage being in two places at once, we can think of this as the viewer's awareness (or consciousness) being in two places at once—at the target, to perceive data; and simultaneously at the viewer's physical location (viewing room) to report data.

Don't be confused—this is not the same as having an out-of-body (OBE) experience. Unlike with OBE, in remote viewing the viewer does not fully "go" to the target as one seems to do in the out-of-body state or in an astral projection (AP) experience. To do so would prevent the viewer from gathering and recording perceptions (data) in real time, as it is being experienced. In OBE or AP, any information or experiential data can only be reported after the experiencer has "returned back" to a "normal state" of awareness. This risks loss of important information due to memory limitations. Contrast this with remote viewing, where the remote viewer records his or her perceptions at the same time as they are being perceived.

5

The viewer is blind to the target, protected from any awareness of the identity or nature of the target or of the tasking used to point the viewer there.

A key principle in remote viewing is that the viewer must have no knowledge of the nature of the target until after the session is completed (single-blind protocol). In most cases, especially in scientific settings, everyone associated with the viewer, such as the session monitor or observers present during the session, must also be unaware of the target (double-blind protocol).

Blinding requires a way to assign the target, which usually involves another person kept separate both from the viewer and from others who might be present during the remote viewing session. This person is responsible for defining the target and creating a way of "pointing" the viewer to the desired target without revealing any information about it. This could involve sealing a reference picture in an envelope and/or defining a verbal tasking cue. Common practice is to assign a code, coordinate, or arbitrary number that functions as a "tasking number," standing in for the target and preventing the viewer from inferring or deducing information about the nature or identity of the target. In remote viewing, the person responsible for making this target assignment is called the "tasker."

6

Remote viewers are aware of and manage the negative effect of mental noise on the remote viewing process.

Due to the fragmentary nature of normal everyday perception, our minds are trained to interpolate available and often disjointed pieces of data to form a "full picture." This function is an important evolutionary survival mechanism, but it can lead to issues in our attempts to perceive information non-locally. Our interpolations are based on previous knowledge and memory. Under normal circumstances, when they interact with newly-perceived data they give us a useful interpretation of what we experience.

But in low-information situations (as remote viewing often is) interpolations may unintentionally result in false interpretations. The viewer's mind attempts to draw conclusions from initially inadequate data, yielding false conclusions. The more limited and fragmentary the available perceptions, the more inaccurate these interpolations become. Because remote viewing is an inexact process, this interpolation mechanism can get in the way of obtaining and recording reliable data during remote viewing sessions.

Remote viewing is the first, and perhaps *only*, psychic discipline that acknowledges the concept of mental noise and has developed ways to address it. The original term for this concept is "Analytical Overlay (AOL)." In some offshoots of the remote viewing methodology, alternative terminology may be used to describe the same concept. Conversely, original CRV terminology (such as ideogram or bilocation) has been imported into other methods, and their original meanings are often altered to represent different concepts. This adds to the confusion about the nature of remote viewing.

7
Remote viewing is a process of description, and not an attempt to "name" or identify the target.

A basic requirement in remote viewing is to *"describe, don't name"* target perceptions. In other words, the most successful viewers use descriptive terms and graphic representations, such as sketches to convey how a target looks, smells, feels, is shaped, sounds, and so on. They avoid labeling or identifying ("naming") the target. This approach helps reduce the analytical processes ("mental noise"—see Principle 6) of the remote viewer.

In reporting remote viewing perceptions, a viewer should describe what he/she perceives, and not try to label it. (For example, instead of "fire truck," a competent viewer will use concepts such as "red, metallic, large, rumbling sounds," and so on. Yet, the target might be something that is red, metallic, large and makes rumbling sounds, but is not actually a firetruck).

Remote viewers are trained to avoid constructing logical "complete stories," and instead focus on collecting descriptive information, including both sensory and conceptual impressions. The task of evaluating a given session and putting the data it contains into context is left to an analyst.

8
Remote viewing involves a defined process, requiring specific protocols.

In this context, "protocols" refers to the conditions under which remote viewing is done, not the method that is used. Among the

THE PRINCIPLES

protocols are several listed in this document, such as blinding conditions (Principle 5); verifiable targets; the requirement for feedback (Principle 11, below); etc. "Defined process," means that the process unfolds within a certain set of boundaries, defined by the protocols.

Remote viewing sessions can be conducted either by the viewer on their own, or with a second person, known as an "interviewer" or "monitor", who assists the viewer with session guidance.

The role of the monitor includes guiding the viewer's focus if necessary, as well as observing the viewer during the session to help them avoid naming and guessing, thereby reducing analytical interference.

In method-based remote viewing, the role of the monitor is augmented by the working structure, which includes a strict placement protocol (often referred to as the "RV method" or "RV protocol") for recording perceptions on paper. This protocol helps to separate raw impressions from analytically processed data, it also differentiates between categories of data, and captures the chronological order in which the perceptions were received.

Similar to how the blinding protocols or the use of a defined written structure for objectification helps the viewer stay on track, when a viewer works solo (that is, without a monitor present to assist) a combination of the aforementioned elements helps in reducing the logical interference or guessing. This at least partially substitutes for the lack of a monitor. In principle, a viewer can work solo and without a written method (e.g., solo-ERV[1]) if they

---

1   ERV = Extended Remote Viewing. In Extended Remote Viewing, or ERV for short, a viewer relaxes on a bed or other comfortable support and tries to reach a "hypnagogic" state–a condition at the borderline between asleep and awake. See glossary at the end of this book.

19

apply other methods of real time data objectification, e.g., using audio or video recordings.

Still, the use of a monitor in RV sessions can be helpful beyond the training process, especially in operational settings where the monitor can help guide the viewer's awareness towards specific perspectives or questions. To maintain the monitor's neutrality and avoid influencing the viewer, there are rules for monitoring, such as monitors being blind (except in a training setting), limited verbal response patterns or a non-intrusion policy. This is to preserve the integrity of the remote viewing session and to ensure that the results are not distorted by external influences.

The task of evaluating remote viewing sessions and putting the data into context is a completely seperate process to remote viewing, and is best performed by a different person, in the role of the analyst.

9

Remote viewing results must be "objectified" (that is, recorded in real-time) in a form objectively accessible to others.

A remote viewer must record all perceptions as they occur, in real time. This is typically done with pen on paper in the form of words and sketches, and/or as an audio recording that is sometimes supplemented by subsequent drawings after the verbal part of the session. 3D modeling can also be part of the objectification process. Kinesthetic interaction with the target, such as sketching and modeling are not just for recording data, but also function to reinforce target contact.

Real time objectification serves many purposes, with a focus on externalizing as much of the viewer's "thinking process" as possible. This not only helps avoid "internal editing" (failing to externalize thoughts and perceptions) but also allows the analyst to track mental noise.

Additionally, the amount of data that can be stored in human short-term memory is too minimal to enable the viewer to transport the full range of perceptions from the remote viewing experience back to the viewing room by memory alone, leading to a potential for massive loss of data and subsequent interpolation—a phenomenon well-known from, for example, the interrogation of witnesses.

10
Procedural and administrative details accompanying the remote viewing process are recorded and tracked.

A remote viewing session transcript will often provide not only the target-relevant perceptual data, but also clues to process-related information concerning the viewer and the session environment, which can aid analysis. This particularly applies to CRV (and its offshoots), which has specific terminology to identify and record this kind of information. But the principle is relevant to any kind of remote viewing, whenever the process is recorded. (Despite obvious benefits, some remote viewing methods do not emphasize this.)

THE PRINCIPLES OF REMOTE VIEWING

11

Post-session feedback is key to the remote viewing process.

As per Ingo Swann's original definition (see above), the availability of feedback is a key element of remote viewing. In this sense, sessions conducted against targets with no verifiable feedback or "ground truth" available are considered speculative psychic work, using some elements of remote viewing protocols but not constituting "full" remote viewing.

Feedback in this context does not mean that every detail about the target is known beforehand (which would render RV useless as an intelligence gathering tool). There can certainly be unknowns. However, the "unknowns" must be embedded within known material to allow for verifiable feedback—for example, to clearly determine through other specific target elements whether the viewer is "on target" or not.

12

Multiple viewers and consensus analysis are essential when applying RV to real-world problems.

Like most other human information collection systems, remote viewing is typically not 100% accurate. In fact, the goal in remote viewing is not to achieve perfection, but rather to maximize the reliability and usefulness of the information gathered. Recognizing sources of interference, such as mental noise, leads to standard practices that help mitigate the effects of inherent inaccuracies in the process. One important technique is to assign multiple viewers to the same task and, after completion of all viewing activities, comparing the results.

This redundant approach serves as an error-correction mechanism, helping to overcome inaccuracies caused and compounded by each individual viewer's encounter with mental noise. Overall reliability of the collected data improves when analysts evaluate each viewer's session data in relation to what the other viewers produced, look for correlations where their data overlap, then placing it into a context where more trustworthy conclusions can be drawn. This work is performed after sessions are complete. It is essential that analysts avoid interfering with the viewing process during sessions.

These principles and practices work together to create a structured approach to remote viewing that aims to maximize the validity and usefulness of the data obtained, while acknowledging and managing the inherent challenges posed by mental noise and the limitations of human perception.

THE PRINCIPLES OF REMOTE VIEWING

PRINCIPLES OF REMOTE VIEWING COMPARISION TO DIFFERENT MODES OF PSYCHIC WORK

	Remote Viewing	OBE / Astral Projection	Clairvoyance	Channeling	Precognition, Visions	Automatic Writing	Constellation Work
Trainable skill **(1)**	●	⊘	⊘	⊘	⊘	●	⊘
Always intentional **(2)**	●	⊘	●	⊘	∅	●	●
Controlled target access **(3)**	●	⊘	●	⊘	∅	●	●
Bilocation balance **(4)**	●	∅	⊘	∅	∅	∅	●
Blinding protocols **(5)**	●	∅	∅	∅	⊘	⊘	⊘
Concept of mental noise **(6)**	●	∅	∅	∅	∅	∅	∅
Descriptive reporting **(7)**	●	∅	∅	∅	∅	∅	∅
Defined working structure **(8)**	●	⊘	∅	●	∅	●	●
Recording in real time **(9)**	●	∅	⊘	●	∅	●	●
Process-related data **(10)**	●	∅	∅	∅	∅	∅	⊘
Feedback **(11)**	●	⊘	⊘	⊘	⊘	⊘	⊘
Redundancy **(12)**	●	∅	⊘	∅	∅	⊘	∅

Chart key: ● yes ∅ no ⊘ partially applied / different versions / not mandatory

Russell Targ and
Hal Puthoff
in front of SRI, 1976

Ingo Swann and his
Military students, in front
of one of Ingo's paintings,
May 1984
(left to right: Bill Ray,
Paul H. Smith, Ed Dames,
Ingo Swann, Charlene
Cavanaugh, Tom McNear)

25

THE PRINCIPLES OF REMOTE VIEWING

Author: CLP © 2024 | Signed by:

—*Experts*

Harold E. Puthoff, Ph.D.
Co-founder and chief scientist, CIA and
DoD-sponsored remote viewing program,
SRI-International, 1972–1985

Russell Targ
Co-founder and scientist,
CIA and DoD-sponsored remote viewing
program, SRI-International, 1972–1984

Skip Atwater
(Cpt., U.S. Army, ret.)
Operations and Training Officer,
Star Gate Remote Viewing Program,
Ft. Meade, Maryland, 1977–1987,
originator of the Military Remote Viewing
Program, former President of The Monroe
Institute (ret.)

Thomas M. McNear
(Lt. Col., U.S. Army, ret.)
Remote Viewer, Trainer and Project Officer,
Star Gate Remote Viewing Program,
Ft. Meade, Maryland, 1982–1985,
first CRV trainee of Ingo Swann

Paul H. Smith, Ph.D.
(Maj., U.S. Army, ret.)
Remote Viewer, Trainer and Project Officer,
Star Gate Remote Viewing Program,
Ft. Meade, Maryland, 1983–1990,
unit historian and longest serving
military/civilian CRV trainer

William G. Ray
(Maj., U.S. Army, ret.)
Remote Viewer, Trainer, Project Manager
and Commander,
Star Gate Remote Viewing Program,
Ft. Meade, Maryland, 1984–1987

THE PRINCIPLES

Jeffrey Mishlove, Ph.D.
Parapsychologist, remote viewing researcher, author, long-time friend of Puthoff and Targ, and others, participant in early RV studies, host of *New Thinking Allowed*

—*Compiled by*

Jana Rogge
Remote Viewer, remote viewing researcher, trainer, author and publisher, co-author of this article, President of the Center Lane Project

—*Endorsers*

John P. Stahler
Remote Viewer, former President of the International Remote Viewing Association (IRVA), Vice President of the Center Lane Project

Jon Noble
Remote Viewer, RV trainer, author, Board member of the Center Lane Project

Lily Fowler
Remote Viewer, professional RV project manager, former Vice President of the International Remote Viewing Association (IRVA), Board member of the Center Lane Project

Hakim Isler
Remote Viewer, martial artist, author and conference speaker, Board member of the Center Lane Project

Shane Ivie
Remote Viewer, creator of Operational Handicapping® (OH), Outreach Associate of the Center Lane Project

Shiva Amini
Remote Viewer, quantum practitioner, Pioneer Member of the Center Lane Project, Community Engagement Lead

27

THE PRINCIPLES OF REMOTE VIEWING

REMOTE VIEWING GLOSSARY

Remote viewing, a practice that explores the boundaries of human perception, has developed a rich lexicon over the decades since its inception. This glossary provides definitions for key terms as originally used by the pioneers of remote viewing at Stanford Research Institute (SRI), including researchers like Hal Puthoff, Russell Targ, and Ingo Swann, as well as other early practitioners.

It's important to note that as remote viewing has evolved, various offshoots and methodologies have emerged, sometimes employing different terminology to describe similar concepts. The definitions presented here focus on the original usage, offering a foundation for understanding the core principles of remote viewing. For a more comprehensive exploration of remote viewing terminology, including contemporary usage and expanded definitions, readers are encouraged to visit the Glossary section on the Center Lane Project website: www.centerlane-rv.org/glossary.

ANALYTICAL OVERLAY (AOL)

In remote viewing, AOL is used as an abbreviation for the term "Analytical Overlay," referring to analytically processed data, e.g., mental noise, speculations, assumptions, etc.

Analytical overlay is the response of the viewer's own imagination to data obtained from the psychic "signal line." As bits of information flow in, any given bit might stimulate a viewer's memories or imagination, and generate a false or misleading impression or image. This impression may spring from a kernel of true information, but a kernel that is soon smothered in a false mental idea or picture. (This is often referred to as "mental noise.")

As an example, let's say the viewer is given the Eiffel Tower as a remote viewing target. The viewer is supposed to be "blind" to the target from the outset, and thus has no conscious awareness of the nature or identity of the target. In the process of acquiring the signal line, the viewer perceives small bits of data at first—in this case, perhaps a girder with rivets in it as part of the target. The viewer's mind remembers that it saw a girder similar to this in a bridge over a local river. The viewer erroneously conjures up the idea of "bridge" in his/her mind. Obviously, the conclusion is wrong, even if the original, core data may have been correct.

Sometimes AOLs may come closer to reflecting the true nature of the target. This is known as AOL/Signal, a form of AOL which in some cases happens to closely match correct aspects of the site. AOL/Signals are often useful for analysis (whereas AOL itself seldom is), so long as some caution is still exercised. Too much reliance on what is reported as AOL/S can lead an analyst astray as well.

Even if AOLs are wrong most of the time, they are not always incorrect. But there is no way for the viewer within a session to make that distinction. The separation of analytically processed data and raw data within a session is therefore an important principle of remote viewing.

APERTURE

Aperture is a term of art in certain remote viewing methodologies, signifying the point or portal through which information transitions from the subconscious into conscious awareness.

ASSOCIATIVE REMOTE VIEWING (ARV)

Associative Remote Viewing (ARV) is a technique that combines remote viewing with outcome prediction for binary events. ARV is not a way of doing remote viewing (not a method). Instead, it is a way of using remote viewing (an application of remote viewing) to obtain a certain kind of information about the future. Any workable method of remote viewing can be used for an ARV project.

In ARV, two distinct targets (often images, but also objects or places) are selected and associated with possible outcomes of a future event, such as stock market movements or sports results. A remote viewer then attempts to describe the target feedback they will be shown in the future, without knowing which outcome it represents. The remote viewing session takes place before the event happens, and the viewer is not informed about the nature of the event or the possible outcomes. After the session, analysts compare the viewer's description to the two selected images to determine which outcome is more likely. Once the actual event occurs, the viewer is shown the target feedback (image or object) associated with the real outcome.

ARV is designed to bypass conscious interference by having viewers describe seemingly unrelated images rather than directly attempting to predict the event itself. This technique has been used for various purposes, including financial market predictions and research studies.

ARV has shown notable success in various experiments. The overall trend suggests that ARV has demonstrated potential as a predictive instrument when applied correctly, though like any predictive method, it is not without risks or failures. The successes have fueled ongoing interest and research in ARV, with numerous attempts yielding favorable outcomes across various predictive domains. Both individuals and organizations have employed ARV for research and profit-seeking purposes, with varying degrees of success reported.

CONTROLLED REMOTE VIEWING (CRV)

Controlled Remote Viewing (CRV) is a structured method developed to perform remote viewing. It involves a step-by-step protocol designed to help viewers distinguish between imagination and genuine intuitive perceptions. The technique uses a written process to organize and record impressions, helping to separate signal from noise in the viewer's mind.

Ten years after the initial start of remote viewing research at SRI-International, in 1981, the way of working changed to a new level, and the CRV protocol known today was developed. CRV—the acronym then stood for "Coordinate Remote Viewing," later redesignated as "Controlled Remote Viewing"—was, in contrast to the methodology previously used, a structured methodological approach based on a multi-stage protocol sequence.

Key players in this development and testing effort were, on the SRI side, "inventors" Hal Puthoff and Ingo Swann, and on the military side, Rob Cowart and Tom McNear, who were the first "official military guinea pigs" in training with this new protocol. Beginning in 1984, a second group of military personnel from Ft. Meade, now in the Center Lane program, trained in the new methodology under the guidance of Ingo Swann.

CENTER LANE

One of the code names of the Military remote viewing programme,

GLOSSARY

covering the 1983–1984 period, the time when Ingo Swann trained 5 Military remote viewers—Tom McNear, Bill Ray, Paul H. Smith, Charlene Cavanaugh (Shufelt) and Ed Dames—in the CRV method that he had developed together with Hal Puthoff.

STAR GATE

Star Gate was the code name for a secret U.S. government program, primarily run by the Defense Intelligence Agency (DIA) and SRI International, that investigated the use of remote viewing for military and intelligence purposes. The program's main activities included both operational intelligence-gathering using trained remote viewers and scientific research into the phenomenon. While the program began in the late 1970s and operated under several different code names over the years, including GRILL FLAME, CENTER LANE, and SUN STREAK, it was only in 1991 that the consolidated project adopted the name "STAR GATE." Today, "Star Gate" is commonly used in public discourse to refer to the entire remote viewing initiative, even though it was originally just the final code name in a series. It was terminated and declassified in 1995.

Program Cover Name	Sponsoring Headquarters	Approx. Dates of Existence
Gondola Wish	Army INSCOM	1977 to 1979
Grill Flame	Army INSCOM (and AMSAA)	1979 to 1983
Center Lane	Army INSCOM	1983 to 1985
Dragoon Absorb	Army INSCOM and DIA	1985 to 1986
Sun Streak	Defense Intelligence Agency (DIA)	1986 to 1990
Star Gate	DIA	1990 to 1995

THE PRINCIPLES OF REMOTE VIEWING

EXTENDED REMOTE VIEWING (ERV)
In the early days of remote viewing research in 1972 at SRI-International (back then Stanford Research Institute), an unstructured methodology and a form of free response interview were used. A similar approach was adopted at the military remote viewing unit located at Ft. Meade under the direction of F. Holmes "Skip" Atwater, where some of today's best known remote viewers worked during the period of the "Grill Flame" project (1977–1983). Preparations and viewer selection were carried out in cooperation with the SRI team. From 1979 onward, the military ran its own operational remote viewing effort.

During this period, the term Extended Remote Viewing (ERV) came into existence, coined by Skip for the military variant of the method, which was based on elements of the original SRI approach ("freeform" RV or Generic Remote Viewing, GRV) incorporating elements and insights from Bob Monroe's research work.

In Extended Remote Viewing, or ERV for short, a viewer relaxes on a bed or other comfortable support and tries to reach a "hypnagogic" state—a condition at the borderline between asleep and awake. (Earlier in ERV's development, Hemi-Sync binaural beat technology was used to help induce this hypnagogic state.) The room is darkened and soundproofed if possible.

As the viewer reaches the edge of consciousness, a second person in the room, the monitor (also known as the "interviewer"), begins the session by quietly giving directions to the viewer to access the desired target. These directions may be a geographic coordinate or some other reference number, instructions to "access and describe" a target sealed in an envelope the monitor has brought along, or even simply the word "target." Once the viewer describes elements of the correct target, the monitor poses questions about it. These questions may request details, purposes, appearances, construction, activities, events, persons, or other target-related information. The monitor writes down or electronically records the answers the viewer provides. After the session the viewer makes additional notes about what was perceived, along with appropriate sketches or drawings.

Remote viewing is based on the theory that RV impressions bubble up from the subconscious. When trying to move subconscious impressions into waking consciousness, "mental noise" often results. This mental noise arises from all the guessing, speculation, remembering, confusion, and so on that seems to regularly a part of every human's mental life. ERV was developed with the idea that deliberately trying to come as close to an unconscious state as one can while still maintaining just enough awareness to respond to the monitor should make it easier to detect subtle remote viewing impressions with less mental noise. Some people feel the ERV approach is helpful, while others report that the noise does not seem any less in ERV than it is in other remote viewing methods.

The term ERV was originally coined by Capt. F. Holmes "Skip" Atwater in the early 1980s while he was operations and training officer for the Army's remote viewing unit at Ft. Meade, MD and was used as a secondary remote viewing method throughout the latter half of the Star Gate Program. ERV existed before its name did, and was used by some of the first military viewers. Because an ERV session took longer than one performed using the controlled remote viewing (CRV) methodology, Atwater decided to call it "extended" remote viewing, and the name stuck. [4]

FEEDBACK

Those responses provided during the session to the viewer to indicate if he has detected and properly decoded site-relevant information; or, information provided at some point after completion of the RV session or project to "close the loop" as it were, providing the viewer with closure as to the site accessed and allowing him to assess the quality of his performance more accurately.

FIRST-TIME EFFECT

In any human activity or skill a phenomenon exists known as "beginner's luck." In remote viewing, this phenomenon is manifest as especially successful performance at the first attempt at psychic functioning, after which the success rate drops sharply, to be built up again gradually through further training. This effect is hypothesized to result from the initial excitation of hereditary but dormant psi-conducting neuronal channels which, when first stimulated by attempted psychoenergetic functioning "catch the analytic system off guard," as it were, allowing high-grade functioning with little other system interference. Once the initial novelty wears off, the analytic systems which have been trained for years to screen all mental functions attempt to account for and control the newly awakened neural pathways, thereby generating increasing amounts of masking "mental noise," or AOL. [5]

GESTALT

The term "gestalt" was first used as part of the terminology of the original CRV protocol. Any given site has an overall nature or "gestalt", as it is referred to below, that makes it uniquely what it is. At the beginning of a remote viewing session, in Stage I, the remote

GLOSSARY

viewer is taught to acquire the signal line, attune himself to it, and proceed to decode and objectify this site gestalt and the major pieces of information that pertain to it.

Major Gestalt: The overall impression presented by all elements of the site taken for their composite interactive meaning. The one concept that more than all others would be the best description of the site. [5]

IDEOGRAM

With the development of Controlled Remote Viewing (CRV) as the first written remote viewing protocol in the early 1980's, the ideogram was introduced as the first step—stage 1—in this method.

In remote viewing, an ideogram is a spontaneous, reflexive mark made on paper at the beginning of a session. Developed by Ingo Swann as part of his Controlled Remote Viewing (CRV) methodology, the ideogram serves as the viewer's first contact with the target's information. It's drawn quickly and involuntarily, without conscious thought or analysis, representing the viewer's initial kinesthetic encounter with the target area and capturing its main "gestalt" or essence. Ideograms act as a physical expression of information received below the threshold of conscious perception. After drawing the ideogram, the viewer interprets it through the "I-A-B" (Ideogram-Analyze-Break down) procedure, describing the motion and feeling associated with creating the mark. Typically unique to each target and viewing session, ideograms don't necessarily resemble the target's physical appearance but rather convey its essential nature. While the original CRV method emphasizes the kinesthetic aspect of ideograms, some modern approaches have developed "lexicon" systems associating specific shapes with

37

particular target types. In both approaches, the ideogram serves as a crucial tool for establishing initial contact with the target information and can significantly influence the subsequent remote viewing session's quality.

MATRIX

Matrix: Something within which something else originates or takes form or develops. A place or point of origin or growth. [5]

The Matrix has been described as a huge, non-material, highly structured, mentally accessible "framework" of information containing all data pertaining to everything in both the physical and non-physical universe. In the same vein as Jung's Cosmic Unconsciousness, the Matrix is open to and comprises all conscious entities as well as information relating to everything else living or nonliving by accepted human definition. It is this informational framework from which the data encoded on the signal line originates. This Matrix can be envisioned as a vast, three dimensional geometric arrangement of dots, each dot representing a discrete information bit. Each geographic location on the earth has a corresponding segment of the Matrix corresponding exactly to the nature of the physical location. When the viewer is prompted by the coordinate or other targeting methodology, he accesses the signal line for data derived from the Matrix. By successfully acquiring (detecting) this information from the signal line, then coherently decoding it through his conscious awareness and faculties, he makes it available for analysis and further exploitation by himself or others.

Remote viewing is made possible through the agency of a hypothetical "signal line." In a manner roughly analogous to standard

GLOSSARY

radio propagation theory, this signal line is a carrier wave which is inductively modulated by its intercourse with information and may be detected and decoded by a remote viewer. This signal line radiates in many different frequencies, and its impact on the viewer's perceptive faculties is controlled through a phenomenon known as "aperture." Essentially, when the remote viewer first detects the signal line in Stage I, it manifests itself as a sharp, rapid influx of signal energy — representing large gestalts of information. In this situation, we therefore speak of a "narrow" aperture, since only a very narrow portion of the signal line is allowed to access the consciousness. In later stages involving longer, slower, more enduring waves, the aperture is spoken of as being "wider."

METHODS

In today's terminology, in Remote Viewing, the term "method" is generally used when referring to the application of a specific written working protocol.

Remote viewer Joe McMoneagle first insisted on a rigid distinction between "method" and "protocol" shortly after remote viewing was declassified in the mid 1990s. Therefore, regardless of the scientific usage, the following definition is common in the world of Remote Viewing: "Method" refers to the specific application (e.g., CRV, TRV, ERV), while "protocol" describes the framework under which the viewer operates (blinding, feedback, etc.). An enlightening article on this can be found here: www.rviewer.com/protocol-or-method-another-remote-viewing-controversy/

In his book, The Essential Guide to Remote Viewing, Paul H. Smith explains his usage: "... Remote viewing [...] is not just a method of

THE PRINCIPLES OF REMOTE VIEWING

using ESP. "Remote viewing" also refers to an experimental protocol. In other words, the framework, rules and procedures within which a remote viewing session is conducted can be considered "remote viewing" as well. There are various remote viewing methods—you can think of "methods" as a set of techniques for how to do remote viewing. Then there is the remote viewing protocol. You can think of protocols as the goals a viewer is supposed to aim for and the conditions under which remote viewing should be done. Take lap swimming as an analogy, for example. There are any number of strokes ("methods") a swimmer can use to get from one end of the pool to the other. But the conditions ("protocols") are the same no matter which stroke is used: there must be water; it must be deep enough; the swimmer must go end-to-end, etc." [6]

MONITOR (INTERVIEWER)

The individual who assists the viewer in a remote viewing session. The monitor provides the coordinate, observes the viewer to help insure he stays in proper structure (discussed below), records relevant session information, provides appropriate feedback when required, and provides objective analytic support to the viewer as necessary. The monitor plays an especially important role in training beginning viewers. [5]

OBJECTIFICATION

Objectification is one of the core principles of RV. (objectify: to present as an object, externalize, to write on paper.) [2]

The act of physically saying out loud and writing down information. Objectification serves several important functions. First, it allows the information derived from the signal line to be recorded and expelled from the system, freeing the viewer to receive further information and become better in tune with the signal line. Secondly, it makes the system independently aware that its contributions have been acknowledged and recorded. Thirdly, it allows re-input of the information into the system as necessary for further prompting. In effect, objectification "gives reality" to the signal line and the information it conveys. Finally, objectification allows non-signal line derived material (inclemencies, AOLs, etc.) that might otherwise clutter the system and mask valid signal line data to be expelled. [5]

OUTBOUNDER/OUT-BOUND EXPERIMENT

What came to be called the "Out-Bound Experimenter" model by SRI, was designed and implemented in 1971–1972, at the American Society for Psychical Research (ASPR), with Ingo Swann as subject, Janet Mitchell as monitor and Karlis Osis and Gertrude Schmeidler as supervisors.

Since the early research at the ASPR and SRI, the Out-Bound Experiment (nowadays titled "Outbounder" or "Beacon" remote viewing) has come into general usage, both in scientific experiments and informal settings. It has also become a popular demonstration at conferences and with groups to showcase the ability to perceive hidden or remote information through anomalous or psychic means. This experimental protocol has gained traction as a method to explore and potentially validate claims of extrasensory perception and remote viewing capabilities.

In an outbounder remote viewing experiment, a remote viewer attempts to describe a distant, randomly selected target location visited by a beacon team, while remaining blind to the target's identity. The process begins with the preparation of multiple distinct

THE PRINCIPLES OF REMOTE VIEWING

target sites, each sealed in identical envelopes to ensure randomness and prevent information leakage. Just before the experiment, a target is chosen at random, and the beacon team travels to that location, while the viewer remains sequestered and unaware of the selection. At a predetermined time, the viewer describes their impressions of the site, often through sketches and verbal reports. After the session, feedback is provided either by taking the viewer to the actual target location or showing a video of it, allowing direct comparison between the viewer's perceptions and the real site. This feedback helps the viewer refine their skills and enables objective assessment of the session's accuracy. The experiment is designed to test whether the presence of a known person (the beacon team) at the site aids the viewer's ability to perceive remote locations, and variations of the protocol may include different timing or target selection methods to enhance experimental rigor.

REMOTE VIEWING

The term Remote Viewing was first coined in 1971 by Ingo Swann and Janet Mitchell, along with Karlis Osis and Gertrude Schmeidler, at the American Society for Psychical Research (ASPR). When Swann was invited in the 1970s to participate in Psi experiments at the Stanford Research Institute (SRI), CA, he took the concept of Remote Viewing with him. The SRI group initially headed by physicist Hal Puthoff, and later joined by Russell Targ and others, implemented Remote Viewing into their experimental protocols.

REMOTE VIEWER ("VIEWER")

The person who perceives and processes the data. Often referred to simply as "viewer," the remote viewer is a person who employs his mental faculties to perceive and obtain information to which he has no other access and of which he has no previous knowledge concerning persons, places, events, or objects separated from him by time, distance, or other intervening obstacles.

SESSION
A work unit that the viewer conducts with pen and paper; an average session lasts between 45 to 120 minutes.

STAGES (IN REMOTE VIEWING)
For the sake of clarity, ease of instruction, and facility of control, the CRV methodology is divided into discreet, progressive "stages," each dealing with different or more detailed aspects of the site. Stage I is the first and most general of the six stages thus far identified. Each stage is a natural progression, building on the information obtained during the previous stage. Each session must start with Stage I, progress on through Stage II, Stage III, and so forth, through the highest stage to be complete in that particular session.

A properly executed Stage I is the very foundation of everything that follows after it, and it is therefore of outmost importance to maintain correct structure and achieve an accurate Stage I concept of the site. All CRV sessions begin with Stage I. [5]

STRUCTURE
The manner in which the mission is to be conducted.

In RV, structure exists to help the viewer to produce the most accurate information—with the least amount of confusion. The viewer learns to focus on the process (correct behavior), not on the outcome.

THE PRINCIPLES OF REMOTE VIEWING

"... In teaching CRV we are not teaching the trainee to be psychic. We are not teaching him to receive the signal. We are teaching him the proper format to be used in objectifying the data he perceives upon receiving the coordinate. This is known as the session "Structure". In this CRV technology we believe that as long as the viewer maintains proper control of his structure the data can be considered generally correct. It must be stressed to the viewer at all times that only by monitoring his structure can he know the value or correctness of the data he is producing. The best results are produced when the viewer ignores the content of the data and concentrates on the structure. This structure is always controlled by the viewer. [...]

Structure is broken into two areas: a) The interaction of the interviewer and viewer and b) the proper sequences of steps taken by the viewer to grasp the ideograms and objectify the data.

Each consecutive entry on the paper is entered below the previous entry. This provides a chronological history of the data. If, during the session it is noted that the viewer is out of structure, this chronological history will allow him to review the data and to correct the structure. At the conclusion of the session, an analyst, by reviewing the session structure, can know the reliability of the data." [5]

"Structure" is a singularly important element in remote viewing theory. The word "structure" signifies the orderly process of proceeding from general to specific in accessing the signal line, of objectifying in proper sequence all data bits and RV-related subjective phenomena [...] and rigorous extraction of AOL from the viewer's system by conscientious objectification. Structure is executed in a formal ordered format sequence using pen and paper.

Structure is the key to usable RV technology. It is through proper structure-discipline that mental noise is suppressed and signal line information allowed to emerge cleanly. As expressed by one early student [Rob Cowart], "Structure! Content be damned!" is the universal motto of the remote viewer. As long as proper structure is maintained, information obtained may be relied on. If the viewer starts speculating about content—wondering "what it is"—he will begin to depart from proper structure and AOL will inevitably result. One of the primary duties of both monitor and viewer is to insure the viewer maintains proper structure, taking information in the correct sequence, at the correct stage, and in the proper manner. [5]

TASKING
Written assignment for the viewer. (The viewer is kept blind to the tasking.)

TASKING NUMBER
Also: coordinate, target reference number (TRN). Each tasking is assigned a sequence of numbers as a neutral address. The viewer receives only this number to begin their work.

TARGET
The defined goal of a tasking or assignment.

GLOSSARY RESOURCES

[1] Center Lane Project. *Glossary*. www.centerlane-rv.org/glossary

[2] McNear, T. (1985, Feb.). *Coordinate remote viewing stages I–VI and beyond* (DIA Report). Defense Intelligence Agency.

[3] McNear, T., Smith, P. H., & Rogge, J. (2023). *The Foundations of Controlled Remote Viewing*. Center Lane Publishing.

[4] Smith, P. H. *rviewer.com*. www.rviewer.com

[5] Smith, P. H. (1986, May). *Coordinate remote viewing (CRV) manual* (DIA Manual). Defense Intelligence Agency.

[6] Smith, P. H. (2015). *The essential guide to remote viewing: The secret military remote perception skill anyone can learn*. Intentional Press.

THE CLP TARGET LIBRARY

At Center Lane Project we have curated remote viewing targets for members of all levels to practice and hone their skills. Our target library is unique in a number of ways.

We offer targets specific to basic, intermediate and advanced levels, allowing for practice on every stage of remote viewing. **While these tiered targets are perfectly geared towards CRV training, they are open to all methodologies!** Every target offers an option to receive in-session Stage 1 feedback, with just a click. We also include special target categories such as "Calibration" to refine your identification of gestalts, or "Fun Targets" which will help you train your AOL handling with unexpected scenarios.

Our targets offer a surplus of feedback, with multiple pictures, aerial maps, geographic coordinates and a descriptive narrative of the target with links for further exploration. Another special feature is the option to download a PDF feedback sheet that can be printed out and stapled to your session.

Safety Vetted: All targets are real-world, carefully selected to avoid highly emotional or esoteric content.

Session Gallery: Members can submit their sessions to be showcased as examples and encouragement for others.

Monthly Updates: A new curated target is added to the library every month.

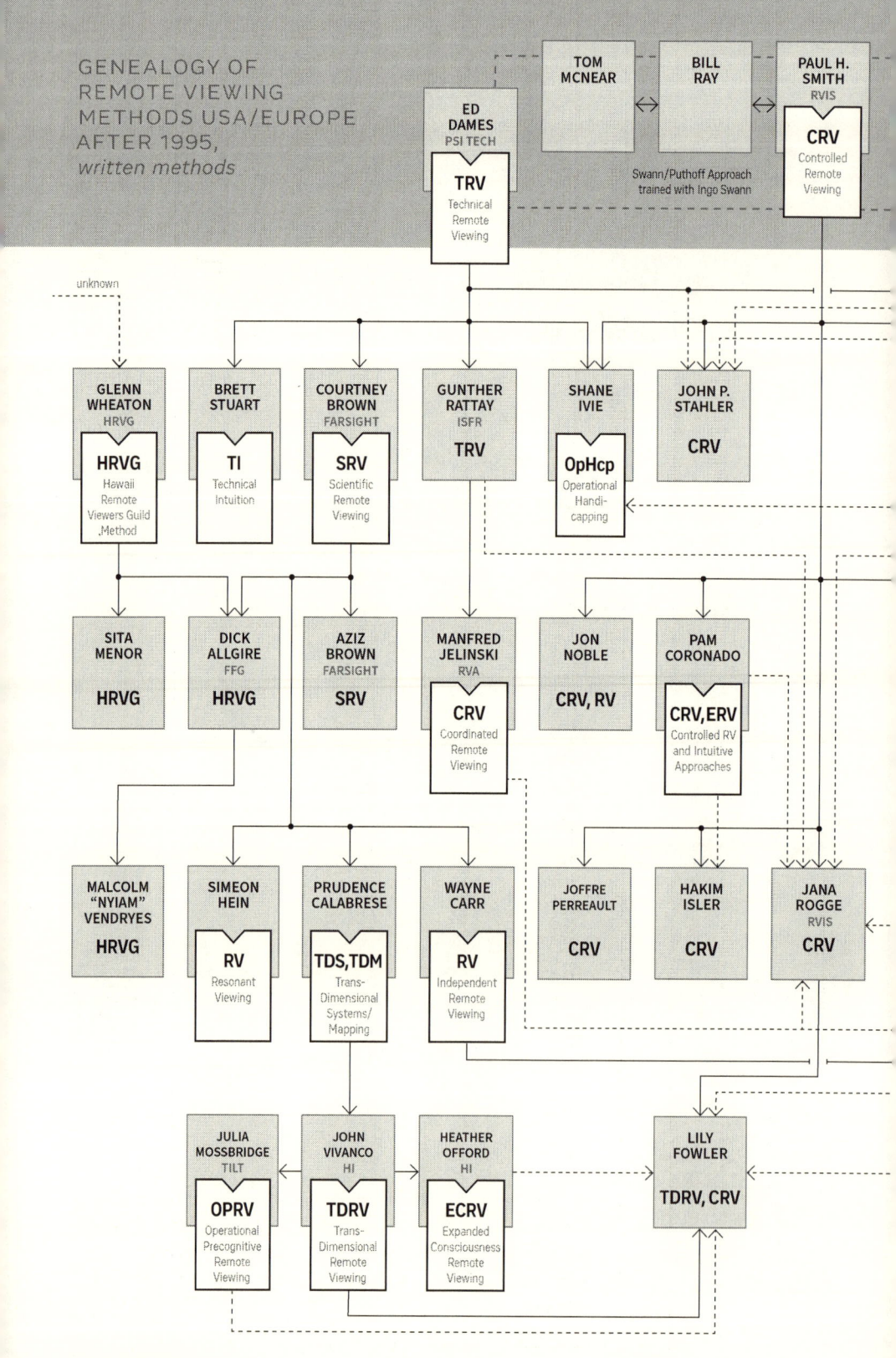

GENEALOGY OF REMOTE VIEWING METHODS USA/EUROPE AFTER 1995,
written methods

TOM MCNEAR

BILL RAY
Swann/Puthoff Approach
trained with Ingo Swann

PAUL H. SMITH
RVIS
CRV
Controlled Remote Viewing

ED DAMES
PSI TECH
TRV
Technical Remote Viewing

unknown

GLENN WHEATON
HRVG
HRVG
Hawaii Remote Viewers Guild Method

BRETT STUART
TI
Technical Intuition

COURTNEY BROWN
FARSIGHT
SRV
Scientific Remote Viewing

GUNTHER RATTAY
ISFR
TRV

SHANE IVIE
OpHcp
Operational Handicapping

JOHN P. STAHLER
CRV

SITA MENOR
HRVG

DICK ALLGIRE
FFG
HRVG

AZIZ BROWN
FARSIGHT
SRV

MANFRED JELINSKI
RVA
CRV
Coordinated Remote Viewing

JON NOBLE
CRV, RV

PAM CORONADO
CRV, ERV
Controlled RV and Intuitive Approaches

MALCOLM "NYIAM" VENDRYES
HRVG

SIMEON HEIN
RV
Resonant Viewing

PRUDENCE CALABRESE
TDS, TDM
Trans-Dimensional Systems/Mapping

WAYNE CARR
RV
Independent Remote Viewing

JOFFRE PERREAULT
CRV

HAKIM ISLER
CRV

JANA ROGGE
RVIS
CRV

JULIA MOSSBRIDGE
TILT
OPRV
Operational Precognitive Remote Viewing

JOHN VIVANCO
HI
TDRV
Trans-Dimensional Remote Viewing

HEATHER OFFORD
HI
ECRV
Expanded Consciousness Remote Viewing

LILY FOWLER
TDRV, CRV

© 2024 JANA ROGGE

```
MILITARY
─────────
CIVIL
```

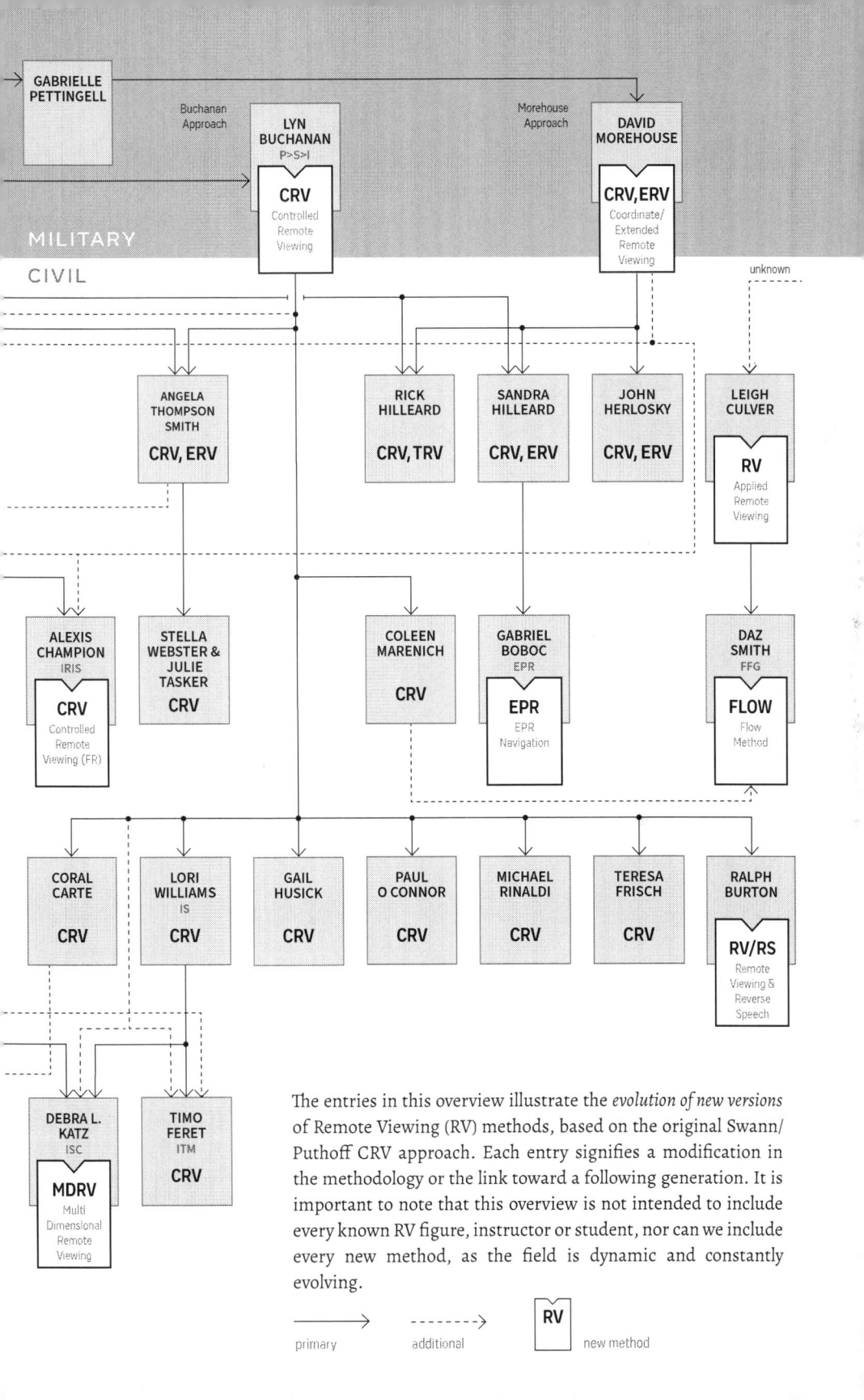

GABRIELLE PETTINGELL

Buchanan Approach → **LYN BUCHANAN** P>S>I
CRV — Controlled Remote Viewing

Morehouse Approach → **DAVID MOREHOUSE**
CRV, ERV — Coordinate/Extended Remote Viewing

ANGELA THOMPSON SMITH
CRV, ERV

RICK HILLEARD
CRV, TRV

SANDRA HILLEARD
CRV, ERV

JOHN HERLOSKY
CRV, ERV

LEIGH CULVER
RV — Applied Remote Viewing

unknown

ALEXIS CHAMPION IRIS
CRV — Controlled Remote Viewing (FR)

STELLA WEBSTER & JULIE TASKER
CRV

COLEEN MARENICH
CRV

GABRIEL BOBOC EPR
EPR — EPR Navigation

DAZ SMITH FFG
FLOW — Flow Method

CORAL CARTE
CRV

LORI WILLIAMS IS
CRV

GAIL HUSICK
CRV

PAUL O CONNOR
CRV

MICHAEL RINALDI
CRV

TERESA FRISCH
CRV

RALPH BURTON
RV/RS — Remote Viewing & Reverse Speech

DEBRA L. KATZ ISC
MDRV — Multi Dimensional Remote Viewing

TIMO FERET ITM
CRV

The entries in this overview illustrate the *evolution of new versions of Remote Viewing (RV) methods*, based on the original Swann/Puthoff CRV approach. Each entry signifies a modification in the methodology or the link toward a following generation. It is important to note that this overview is not intended to include every known RV figure, instructor or student, nor can we include every new method, as the field is dynamic and constantly evolving.

⟶ primary   ---⟶ additional   **RV** new method

printed in 2025
Center Lane Books
CENTER LANE PUBLISHING
Jana Rogge, Germany
Email: online@janarogge.de

Copyright © 2025
The Center Lane Project

All rights reserved. No part of this publication may be reproduced, distributed, or transmitted in any form or by any means, including reprography and computer processing, without the prior written permission of the publisher, except in the case of brief quotations embodied in critical reviews and certain other noncommercial uses permitted by copyright law.

Layout and overall design: Jana Rogge
Cover graphic based on
a graphic by alisaaa, AdobeStock.com

ISBN 978-3-911151-08-5

Made in the USA
Middletown, DE
20 September 2025